RUDOLF STEINER (1861–1925) called his spiritual philosophy 'anthroposophy', meaning 'wisdom of the human being'. As a highly developed seer, he based his work on direct knowledge and perception of spiritual dimensions. He initiated a modern and universal 'science of spirit', accessible to anyone willing to exercise clear and unprejudiced thinking.

From his spiritual investigations Steiner provided suggestions for the renewal of many activities, including education (both general and special), agriculture, medicine, economics, architecture, science, philosophy, religion and the arts. Today there are thousands of schools, clinics, farms and other organizations involved in practical work based on his principles. His many published works feature his research into the spiritual nature of the human being, the evolution of the world and humanity, and methods of personal development. Steiner wrote some 30 books and delivered over 6000 lectures across Europe. In 1924 he founded the General Anthroposophical Society, which today has branches throughout the world.

SELF-KNOWLEDGE
THE JOURNEY TO WISDOM

*Higher Knowledge, the Guardian of the Threshold
and the Power of Christ*

RUDOLF STEINER

Selected and compiled by Andreas Neider

RUDOLF STEINER PRESS

Translated by Matthew Barton

Rudolf Steiner Press,
Hillside House, The Square
Forest Row, RH18 5ES

E-mail: office@rudolfsteinerpress.com

www.rudolfsteinerpress.com

Published by Rudolf Steiner Press 2015

Originally published in German under the title *Erkenne dich selbst* by
Rudolf Steiner Verlag, Basel, in 2010

A catalogue record for this book is available from the British Library

Print book ISBN: 978 1 85584 412 4
Ebook ISBN: 978 1 85584 453 7

Cover by Morgan Creative
Typeset by DP Photosetting, Neath, West Glamorgan
Printed and bound in Great Britain by 4edge Limited, Essex

Contents

About this Book

If we engage more fully with anthroposophy we will discover two things initially. First, anthroposophy is not a doctrine or set of dogmas but a path towards deeper insights supported by the countless suggestions, exercises and meditations that Rudolf Steiner gave. Secondly, we find, however, that astonishingly few of those who have been involved in anthroposophy since Steiner's day have arrived at their own independently acquired spiritual insights by pursuing this path.

Instead, from time to time, there have been individuals who presented somewhat dubious spiritual perceptions relating, say, to former incarnations or encounters with spiritual beings—the latter offering diverse messages to the individuals in question. Anyone who has a fleeting or superficial encounter with anthroposophy may well be inclined therefore to turn away from it again. But if we do not allow ourselves to be misled by such things, we will sooner or later find the underlying reasons for them.

Study of and preoccupation with anthroposophic spiritual science, and in particular carrying out the relevant exercises and meditations, starts to change our relationship with the world we perceive around us. In the visible physical world we are used to experiencing ourselves as separate from surrounding objects and phenomena. As we begin to have spiritual perceptions however—initially appearing in imaginative form and thus in pictures or images—we will inevitably find that these are not separate from our interior life but arise from and are influenced by it.

Here we discover the fundamental distinction between spiritual and sensory perception. With the latter, given the tangible reality of objects outside me, I can always distinguish between what I am myself and the outer object. In the case of spiritual perceptions by contrast, it is far less easy to distinguish between the productions of my own psyche and real spiritual entities. In fact, most objections to anthroposophy cast doubt on our capacity to perceive spiritual worlds at all.

Objections of this kind, however, are ultimately only barriers thrown up by ourselves to hinder our access to worlds of spirit. In the meditative texts compiled here, Rudolf Steiner shows us that, as we begin to know ourselves more fully, we can indeed approach the threshold to spiritual realities.

'Man know thyself' was the ancient Greek instruction to those who sought higher knowledge. Whoever wishes to gain spiritual insights has to learn to distinguish between what belongs to his own being or nature and what is part of his real spiritual environment. But as long as we draw back from this self-knowledge we will either gain only dubious spiritual perceptions—since it is unclear what the person concerned has himself introduced into these—or will have no such perceptions in the first place.

But why do we draw back in some alarm from insight into our own being? Answering this question brings us to one of the most important things that the meditant can gain from the texts gathered here:

You see, we have something within us that obstructs a deeper knowledge of ourselves. This is an urge that arises when we must acknowledge a characteristic trait in ourselves, *and have no wish to allow any illusion to intrude*, to reshape, reform this characteristic. If we do not heed this urge, but simply divert our attention from ourselves and remain as we are, we naturally also deprive ourselves of the means to perceive this particular quality in us. But if we penetrate our own nature, and become aware of this or that characteristic without illusion, we will either find we are able to improve it or will be unable to do so at our present stage of life. In the latter case, a feeling will insinuate itself into our soul that we must call a sense of shame.[1]

A feeling of shame always arises when we seek to hide from the gaze of the outer world something that we find disagreeable. Rudolf Steiner goes on to point out that a kind of hidden sense of shame exists in relation to self-knowledge: 'This concealed feeling, though, works in a way similar to the more apparent kind we ascertained in ordinary life: it prevents our inmost being appearing to others in a perceptible picture.'[2] This also explains why, in the absence of the necessary self-knowledge, we cannot gain access to spiritual perception:

> Since a person's own inner being is concealed from him, he cannot perceive what would allow him to develop the means or tools for perceiving the soul-spiritual world; he is unable to reconfigure his being in a way that enables it to acquire spiritual organs of perception.[3]

Thus the kind of self-knowledge we are speaking of here seems an essential precondition for any form of higher knowledge. When we really engage fully with it, it can seem an awkward or unpleasant thing, since '. . . if we penetrate our own nature, and become aware of this or that characteristic without illusion, we will either find we are able to improve it or will be unable to do so at our present stage of life.'[4]

In the latter case a sense of resignation—a great danger in this form of self-knowledge—might easily arise:

> As we enter the world of spirit, an aspect of self-knowledge comes about—as our first supersensible achievement—of which previously we can have had scarcely any inkling. And we discover all that we must leave behind if we really wish to enter with full knowledge into the world in which we are actually always immersed. There rises before the inner gaze a very sharp and clear awareness of what we have so far made of ourselves as a human being, both consciously and unconsciously, in the sensory world. Such an experience can often lead to us relinquishing all further efforts to penetrate supersensible worlds. You see, we also gain insight here into how we have to learn to feel and sense things differently if our sojourn in the spiritual world is to be successful.[5]

The soul's fundamental powers of morality—as described for instance in chapter 4 of this book—need to be strengthened for us to avoid giving up at this point. The path to higher knowledge is unavoidably connected with this. The certainty that working on the moral underpinning of our own inner life is the only thing that will enable us to confront our own psyche *without any illusion* is at the same time a strong motivating force in engaging with this work of self-knowledge.

Rudolf Steiner adds:

> Far too much is said theoretically and philosophically about self-knowledge. This in fact tends to distract our inner gaze from the serious nature of what is involved here. Yet above and beyond all such seriousness, we can feel profound satisfaction at the thought that human nature is such that it instinctively refrains from entering the world of spirit before becoming able to develop the right degree of self-aware maturity. What profound satisfaction, too, that our initially most significant encounter with a being of the world of spirit is with our own true being, which we must further develop as part of humanity's evolution.[6]

Our sense of impotence when we approach the threshold to the world of spirit, the way we draw back in fear from true self-knowledge and from facing ourselves, are experiences that, ultimately, proceed from an entity Steiner calls the 'Guardian of the Threshold'. He appears to us initially in a form that mirrors the imperfections of our own being. As long as we are not yet ready or willing to work at transforming ourselves, we cannot cross the threshold to the world of spirit and are repulsed.

All this can point us to a fundamental reality of human life on earth that Christian theology calls the 'Fall'. The legend of paradise, the garden of Eden, as related in Genesis, describes the temptation we succumbed to at the beginning of human evolution, as embodied by Lucifer in the form of the serpent who offers Eve the apple from the Tree of Knowledge.

This temptation appears to us simultaneously as gain and loss. Human intellect—the search for knowledge—had to be paid for by the loss of paradise. The human freedom that arose in consequence of us leaving paradise at the same time contains our potential for error and for entanglement in the weight of earthly travails. Freedom always also signifies not only doing what is right, true and good, but the capacity to choose what is wrong, untrue and evil. This potential that we all bear within us derives from the 'Fall'.

The path of self-knowledge as offered here in texts by Rudolf Steiner, inevitably confronts anyone who wishes to pursue this path with the consequences of this 'Fall'. In the pictorial language of the Old Testament, the 'Guardian of the Threshold' can be seen as the angel who stands at the threshold of paradise and repulses our efforts to return there. A person seeking self-knowledge is confronted with the full force of these consequences:

> Consciousness clings to the way in which it can experience itself within the world of senses. There it feels itself in its element, experiencing itself in thoughts, feelings and affects etc. that it owes to the sensory world. We can see how determinedly our awareness clings to these experiences the moment we really enter worlds of spirit. In the same way that we cling to fond memories at certain moments of our life, so at the moment we enter supersensible worlds all the

inclinations we are capable of necessarily arise from our depths of soul; we become aware how we rely fundamentally on the life that connects us with the sensory world.

This dependency appears here in its full reality, without any of the illusions we otherwise form about it during life. As we enter the world of spirit, an aspect of self-knowledge comes about—as our first supersensible achievement—of which previously we can have had scarcely any inkling. And we discover all that we must leave behind if we really wish to enter with full knowledge into the world in which we are actually always immersed. There rises before the inner gaze a very sharp and clear awareness of what we have so far made of ourselves as human being, both consciously and unconsciously, in the sensory world.[7]

But something else is connected with the 'Fall' as well. In Christian tradition, humanity was not left alone, left to its own fate, after being driven from paradise. Divine powers sent the Christ, who liberated human beings again from the entanglement to which they succumbed through the 'Fall'.

For Rudolf Steiner too, the Christ event is the key moment of Earth evolution. However, instead of describing it as a general kind of redemption or forgiveness of sins, he shows clearly that Christ does not relieve us of our karma, of our need to bear our destiny through many earthly lives, but simply prevents the consequences of our deeds having a negative repercussion for the objective world order. In a sense he protects the evolution of the cosmos from the consequences of individual transgressions. As such he is the 'lamb' who takes the 'sins of the world' upon himself.

But Christ does have a central, if initially hidden, importance for our individual striving for self-knowledge. This comes to the fore in the texts in chapter 2 of this book, which reveal how the path of self-knowledge can lead to us experiencing particular scenes that are also described in the Gospels. In this respect, the authors of the Gospels turn out to be people who themselves underwent a process of self-knowledge and who were able to relate such experiences to events at the time of Christ.

As such the meditant can become aware of Christ no longer as a merely legendary figure of dubious reality, due to the questionable nature of the Gospels, but as a real power directly connected with his search for self-knowledge and self-development. Then, accounts of Christ in the Gospel become the outer testimony of an inwardly experienced reality, which the mystic Angelus Silesius expresses in the following words:

> The Cross of Golgotha cannot set us free
> From evil when not raised in you and me.

Our search for self-knowledge thus increasingly appears to us as a path which Christian mysticism describes as that of *Imitatio*, of following in Christ's footsteps. Here we follow him on a path that overcomes the Fall, to perfect our human nature and strengthen its weakness and frailty. Through his life on earth, Christ gave humanity the potential to emulate what he reveals as the archetype of the human being. Angelus Silesius shows us that living in emulation of Christ also involves 'dying into him'; and in his account of the encounter with the 'Guardian of the Threshold', Rudolf Steiner describes this process in a way that relates and corresponds to the nature of modern human beings.

Something further, too, can be achieved through the path of self-knowledge outlined here. The spiritual form in which the human being himself appears in the encounter with the 'Guardian of the Threshold' is described by Rudolf Steiner as the 'double'. All of us bear such a double within us, which, as a kind of unconscious aspect of our own memory, possesses an autonomy divorced from the latter. As soon as we start to perceive supersensibly through spiritual schooling, and refrain from all illusion, the figure of the double appears before us. However, it not only reveals aspects of our current life on earth but in a sense opens the 'account book' of all previous lives on earth, and hence is anything other than an easily endurable experience.

Nevertheless, a person who strives—in particular in a first, fumbling way—for higher knowledge will repeatedly need to acknowledge aspects of his own double and thereby gain deep insight into his own flaws and imperfections. Yet in accepting that he cannot immediately eradicate these flaws he will develop a certain composure in regard to himself, a certain tolerance, that goes hand in hand with a loving persistence in seeking to overcome his weaknesses.

If this happens to a sufficient degree, the social experience of the person in question can undergo a significant change: he develops a completely different view of the weaknesses and errors of others. In ordinary life we remain unaware of the shadow side of our own nature; although it is always present, it cannot be consciously perceived. In social encounters, however, this very fact frequently leads us to perceive and criticize in others the flaws and weaknesses that we ourselves contain within us as double. As soon as we become aware of our own double, we will endure the flaws and weaknesses of those around us with greater composure, or indeed with gestures of loving devotion. Henceforth we will have a different perception of the person whose flaws we have previously criticized, seeking to support and aid him in overcoming them.

In this way the path of self-knowledge begins to bear fruit—however small initially—for social interaction. While the difficulty of persevering on this self-chosen path may often make us despondent, the gains we perceive in our interpersonal relations can, at the same time, offer a certain comfort or consolation.

A further insight sustains us in this process: that in humanity's evolution there is a being willing to endure and take upon himself the weaknesses, flaws and imperfections of *all* human beings:

> We would have to endure unspeakable suffering together if a being had not united with the earth who can undo all we have inflicted upon it, and are no longer capable of altering. This being is the Christ. He does not relieve us of our subjective karma, but removes the spiritually objective effects of our actions, of our culpability. This is, as I have said, what we must pursue further in our soul and sensibility. Only then will we understand that, basically, the Christ is the being con-

nected with the whole of humanity—for, you see, the earth is there for humanity's sake, and thus Christ is connected also with the whole earth. And this is our human weakness, arising from the luciferic temptation: that we are capable of redeeming our karma in a subjective sense, but could not redeem the earth as well. It is the cosmic being Christ who accomplishes this.[8]

Christ united with all humanity, taking its flaws and weaknesses upon himself to ensure that the further course of earth's evolution was not rendered impossible. In this respect, too, the path of self-knowledge leads us to follow in the footsteps of Christ by learning not only to perceive and overcome our own flaws and weaknesses but at the same time to lovingly bear with the flaws and weaknesses of those around us.

However, self-knowledge—as we see in the last two chapters of our selection—also leads us to the realization that our own true higher being, our I, is only at work in us until the age of three, from then on remaining, in a sense, in the world of spirit. According to Rudolf Steiner, therefore, seeking this true I within ourselves actually leads nowhere. Instead we must seek it in our human surroundings—in what comes towards us from others as our destiny:

> Inwardly we are hollow in relation to the reality of our I. All of us are inwardly hollow, and we ought really to acknowledge this. If we review our life in a really honest and truthful way, we will find that the influences exerted on us by others are a great deal more important than what we have supposedly achieved by our own devices.

Human beings today acquire extraordinarily little themselves unless they gain knowledge from super-sensible sources. On outward paths—with no need to be clairvoyant for this purpose—people today are com-pelled to engage with each other socially because they really only exist in others, in their relationship to the other.[9]

The path of self-knowledge therefore leads us not only to increasingly understand our own imperfections and find ways of overcoming them, but also enhances our interest in fellow human beings since we only exist in a real sense in relationship to them. Christ gives me my intrinsically human nature where I am willing to seek it in the encounter with other people.

All supersensible knowledge requires me to meet my own spiritual being, and yet the path of self-knowledge leads me to other people. Thus we experience a kind of reversal of the focus of our quest for insight, learning to perceive ourselves increasingly in the encounter with others, yet drawing increasingly from within ourselves all spiritual perception of the world around us. We become the object of our own observation, and study the world by observing it within us.

Spiritual research is self-enquiry—and this is a further insight we can gain through self-knowledge. The fruits of this path may appear unspectacular initially, yet they are of real benefit. This compilation closes with the thought that every insight of this nature is newly created—something which, in our spiritual search and enquiry, we add as a new element to the world, however minor.

The texts compiled here of course only present a limited excerpt from spoken and written accounts by Rudolf Steiner relating to the question of self-knowledge.[10] The compiler has arranged these passages in a sequence that seems meaningful to him, and trusts that these meditative texts will offer ongoing support and guidance to those who pursue the often intricate and arduous path of self-knowledge.

Andreas Neider
Epiphany 2010

1. The Importance of Self-knowledge for Acquiring Higher Knowledge

At a certain stage as he rises into worlds of higher knowledge, the spiritual pupil notices that the powers of his personality cohere in a different way from their configuration in the physical, sensory world. In the latter, the I gives rise to a unified integrity of his soul faculties—of thinking, feeling and will initially. These three powers of the soul always retain a certain interrelationship in ordinary life. For instance, you see something in the world around you that either pleases or displeases you. In other words, there is a certain inevitability in how the idea of the thing you perceive is associated with a feeling of pleasure or displeasure. It might be that you desire to possess the thing, or perhaps feel motivated to change it in some way or other. Thus your desire and will connect with an idea and a feeling. This companionable connection is caused by the I that brings the idea (thinking), feeling and will into a unity, and by this means creates order between our individual faculties. This *healthy* order would be disrupted if the I did not possess the power to do this—for instance if desire parted company from feeling or thought. Someone who thought a certain thing was right yet wanted to do something knowing it was not right would be in an unhealthy frame of mind. The same would be true if someone did not wish for what he likes but what he dislikes. But as we rise to higher knowledge we find that thinking, feeling and will do actually come asunder, so that each of these faculties acquires a certain independence. Thus a certain thought no longer self-evidently connects with a certain feeling or impulse of will. It turns out instead that we can perceive something truly in our thinking but then, to form any feeling or resolve of will, we need a renewed impetus that we develop by our own means. During supersensible contemplation, thinking, feeling and will do not remain as three powers emanating from the common I-centre of the personality but instead become autonomous entities, three different personalities if you like; and then we must strengthen the I all the more since it no longer has to simply order these three faculties but must guide and direct three *beings*. But this division must only occur during supersensible contemplation; and once again we see here how important it is to accompany the exercises for higher schooling with those which anchor and consolidate our sound capacity for judgement, and strengthen our life of feeling and will. Devoid of this in the higher world we will soon find that the I is too weak and cannot properly guide thinking, feeling and will. If this weakness prevailed the soul would be pulled in different directions as though by three different personalities, losing its inner coherence. But when the spiritual pupil's development unfolds in the right way, this reconfiguration of our faculties represents real progress. The I remains master of the autonomous entities that now form his psyche. As his development continues this process intensifies. The thinking that has become independent causes a particular, fourth soul-spiritual entity to appear, and we can regard this as the direct influx into us of streams that resemble thoughts. The whole world appears here as thought edifice, standing before us like the realm of plants or animals in the physical, sensory domain. Likewise, feeling and will that have become autonomous elicit two powers in the soul that act there as autonomous beings. And they are joined by a seventh power and entity which resembles our own I itself.

This whole experience is connected with another. Before entering the supersensible world, a person knows thinking, feeling and will only as inner soul experience; but as soon as he steps into the supersensible realm, he perceives things that do not express sensory, physical realities but soul-spiritual ones. Behind the qualities of this new world which he perceives, soul-spiritual beings now stand, presenting themselves to him as an external world in the same way that stones, plants and animals appear to his senses in physical, sensory reality. But the spiritual pupil can discover a significant difference between the soul-spiritual world now opening before him and the one he has been used to perceiving through his physical senses. A plant in the sense-perceptible world remains as it is whatever the human soul may feel or think about it. This is not initially so in the case of the images in the world of soul and spirit, which change depending on how we feel or think. Thus we inform them with a quality that proceeds from our own being. If a certain picture appears before us in the world of Imagination, it will assume a particular form if we relate to it with inner indifference; but the moment we feel pleasure or displeasure in regard to it, its form changes. In other words, such images do not initially express only something that has an independent existence outside us but also reflect the nature of the person himself. They are imbued and pervaded by a person's own nature which overlays these entities like a veil. Though a real being stands before us, we do not discern it but see rather what we ourselves engender. Thus we can have something very real before us yet see it falsely. This is not just the case as regards what we notice about ourselves; everything in our own being works upon this world before us. For instance, a person may have hidden inclinations that do not surface in ordinary life because of education and character, but they work upon the soul-spiritual world, which consequently acquires a distinctive colouring through the person's whole being—irrespective of how much he knows or does not know about his own nature and being. In order to advance further beyond this level of development, we have to learn to distinguish between ourselves and the external realm of spirit. We must learn to extinguish all the effects upon the surrounding soul-spiritual world that proceed from ourselves. The only way to do this is by acquiring insight into all that we ourselves foist upon the new world. We therefore first have to have true, thorough self-knowledge before we can perceive our soul-spiritual surroundings with clear vision. In fact, certain realities of human development mean that such self-knowledge *inevitably* arises when we enter the higher world. In the ordinary physical, sensory world we develop our I, our sense of self, and this I acts as a focus of attraction for all that belongs to us. You can say that all our appetites, sympathies, antipathies, passions and enthusiasms, opinions and so forth cohere around this I. And this I is also the focal point for what we call our human karma. If we saw this I unveiled, we would discern how certain types of destiny will inevitably come to meet it in this and subsequent incarnations, depending on how it has lived in previous incarnations, and on what it has acquired during them. This I, along with all that attaches to it, *has* to appear before the human soul as the first image when this soul rises into the world of soul and spirit. In accordance with a law of the world of spirit, this double of the human being must appear before us as our first impression in that world. We can easily understand this fundamental law if we consider the following. In physical, sensory life we only perceive ourselves in so far as we inwardly experience ourselves in our thinking, feeling and will. But this perception is an inner one and does not appear before us like stones, plants or animals. Added to this is the fact that we only become partially acquainted with ourselves through such inward perception. You see, we have something within us that obstructs a deeper knowledge of ourselves. This is an urge that arises when we must acknowledge a characteristic trait in ourselves, *and have no wish to allow any illusion to intrude*, to reshape, reform this characteristic.

If we do not heed this urge, but simply divert our attention from ourselves and remain as we are, we naturally also deprive ourselves of the means to perceive this particular quality in ourselves. But if we penetrate our own nature, and become aware of this or that characteristic without illusion, we will either find we are able to improve it or will be unable to do so at the present stage of our life. In the latter case, a feeling will insinuate itself into our soul that we must call a sense of shame. Our healthy nature is at work here in fact, experiencing various forms of shame through the self-knowledge it acquires. In ordinary life already, this feeling has a very specific effect. Someone who thinks in a healthy way will ensure that the quality in him that fills him with this feeling does not come to outward expression in actions. So shame is a power that prompts us to enclose something within us and not allow it to become outwardly perceptible. If we reflect carefully on this we will see why spiritual research ascribes far deeper effects still to an inner soul experience very closely related to this feeling of shame. It discovers in the hidden depths of the soul a kind of *concealed* shame of which we are unaware in the physical life of the senses, but which acts in a way similar to the tangible sense of shame we know in ordinary life: it prevents our inmost being and nature appearing before us in a perceptible image. If this feeling did not exist we would be confronted with a perception of what we truly are; we would not only inwardly experience our thoughts, feelings and will but perceive them objectively in the same way we see stones, plants and animals. This feeling thus conceals us from ourselves, at the same time veiling the whole soul-spiritual world. You see, since our own inner being is veiled from us we also cannot perceive the means in us for developing the tools to recognize the soul-spiritual world; we cannot reconfigure our being in such a way that it acquires spiritual organs of perception.

But when, by following a proper path of schooling, we work to acquire these organs of perception, the first impression we receive is that of our true nature. We perceive our double. This self-perception cannot be separated from that of the rest of the soul-spiritual world. In ordinary life this feeling of concealed shame works in such a way that it closes before us the door to the soul-spiritual world. If we try to take even a step towards penetrating this world, the sense of unconscious shame immediately conceals the part of the world of spirit that is about to come to our awareness. But the exercises described open up this world. It is indeed the case that this concealed feeling acts in a very benign way. You see, all our power of judgement, feelings and character acquired without spiritual-scientific schooling do not by themselves equip us to endure a perception of our own true nature. If we perceived this unprepared we would lose all sense of self, self-confidence and self-awareness. To ensure this does not happen is the task of the measures we undertake alongside the exercises for higher knowledge to consolidate our healthy power of judgement, our feeling life and our character. In proper schooling, a person will learn a great many unforeseen things from spiritual science, but at the same time he will acquire all the means of self-knowledge and self-observation needed to encounter his double and cope with this. When this comes about, the spiritual pupil will only be seeing in a different form, as picture in the world of Imagination, what he has already come to know in the physical world. If we have first understood the law of karma through our rational faculty in the physical world, we will not be particularly alarmed when we now find the living seeds of our destiny inscribed in the picture of our double. If we have first acquainted our-selves with the evolution of the cosmos and humanity by our ordinary power of judgement, and know that at a certain point in this evolution the powers of Lucifer entered the human soul, we will not find it hard to endure the sight of these luciferic beings, with all their effects, at work in the image of our own being. But here too we can see how necessary it is that we do not demand entry to the spiritual world before understanding certain truths about the world of spirit through our ordinary power of judgement as this develops in the physical, sensory world. As necessary preparation for seeking to enter supersensible worlds, in the proper course of schooling the spiritual pupil should have first learned what is presented in this book before the section on 'Knowledge of Higher Worlds'.

In a schooling that pays no attention to the sureness of a person's faculty of judgement, and the stability of his feelings and character, the pupil can have higher experiences before developing the necessary inner faculties to encounter them properly. In this case his meeting with the double would burden him and lead to errors. And if a person avoided this encounter altogether—which is possible in some circumstances—and were led into the supersensible world without it, he would be quite unable to perceive the true nature and form of this world. You see, he would be quite unable to distinguish between what he projects onto things there and what they really are. It is only possible to make this distinction if one perceives the image of one's own actual being and thereby detaches from the spiritual environment all that flows from one's own inner life. For life in the physical, sensory world, the double is immediately rendered invisible by the sense of shame we have described when we approach the soul-spiritual world, and which at the same time conceals this whole world too. He stands before this whole world like a 'guardian' to prevent entry by those not yet fitted for it. He can therefore be called the 'Guardian of the Threshold to the soul-spiritual world'. We meet this Guardian of the Threshold not only when we enter the world of spirit as described, but also at death. And in the life between death and a new birth he gradually reveals himself during the course of our soul-spiritual development. But our encounter with him there cannot burden us since we are then aware of worlds other than the one we know between birth and death.

If a person were to gain entry to the soul-spiritual world without encountering the 'Guardian of the Threshold', he might well succumb to one illusion after another, since he could never distinguish between what he himself brings into this world and what really belongs to it. Correct schooling must take the spiritual pupil only into the realm of truth and not that of illusion. The encounter with the Guardian must necessarily follow by the very nature of proper schooling, since this encounter itself is an indispensable precaution against the risk of illusion and phantasm when observing supersensible worlds. One of the most essential undertakings of any spiritual pupil is to work carefully on himself to avoid indulging in fantasy, and prevent himself succumbing to illusion or self-deception (suggestion and auto-suggestion). Where guidance for spiritual schooling is carefully followed, the sources of illusion are eradicated. Here it is of course not possible to describe in full detail all the required measures, but only to give a general idea of what is involved. The kinds of illusion to be considered here arise from two sources, first from the way in which we tinge reality with our own psyche. In ordinary life in the sense-perceptible world the risk from this source of illusion is relatively small since here the external world will always impress its reality clearly upon our perception, however the observer seeks to colour it in accordance with his wishes and interests. The moment we enter the world of imaginative reality, however, its pictures are changed by our desires and interests, and it is like having before us a reality which we ourselves have first formed or at least helped to form. But by encountering the Guardian of the Threshold, and acquainting ourselves with all that is within us and which we can therefore carry with us into the soul-spiritual world, we remove this source of illusion. And the preparation which the spiritual pupil engages in before entering the world of soul and spirit has the effect of accustoming him to exclude himself when observing the sense-perceptible world, instead allowing its phenomena and processes to speak to him through their own intrinsic nature alone. Anyone who practises this sufficiently in preparation can calmly await his encounter with the Guardian of the Threshold; and when this encounter occurs he will finally be able to ascertain whether he now genuinely feels capable of leaving his own being to one side when standing before the world of soul and spirit.

The second source of illusion arises when we wrongly interpret an impression we perceive. A simple instance of such illusion in ordinary life is that of sitting in a train and believing that the trees outside are moving in an opposite direction from the train. In fact it is only we ourselves who are moving. There are numerous kinds of illusion in the sense-perceptible world that are harder to correct than this simple instance, but within this world we do find the means to correct them by using our healthy common sense to elicit an explanation. *Reality* is not altered by our misperception. The moment we enter supersensible realms, by contrast, and try to observe a supersensible process but do so with mistaken judgement we foist this mistake upon it; and it becomes so interwoven with the reality there that it cannot immediately be distinguished from it. The error is no longer just in the observer, while the reality is outside him, but the error itself becomes part of the external reality, and therefore cannot simply be corrected by unprejudiced observation. Thus we find a source of ever-burgeoning error, of illusion and fantasy, for anyone who approaches the supersensible world without due preparation. Now just as the spiritual pupil acquires the capacity to exclude illusions arising when his own nature colours supersensible phenomena, so likewise he must achieve the other capacity necessary to inactivate the second characteristic source of illusion. He can exclude what comes from himself by first perceiving the picture of his own double; and he can avoid the second source of error by developing the ability to perceive, *by the very nature and quality* of a supersensible phenomenon, whether it is reality or illusion. If illusions were identical with realities, this distinction would not be possible. But this is not so. Illusions in the supersensible world have *intrinsic* properties which distinguish them from realities. And the spiritual pupil has to know the distinctive characteristics of realities. It seems self-evident to anyone unfamiliar with spiritual schooling to wonder what possible safeguard there can be against illusion since there are so many possible sources of it. He may well ask whether any spiritual pupil can be sure that all his supposed higher perceptions are not based on illusion and self-deception. But this view fails to take account of the fact that all proper spiritual schooling, and the very way in which this unfolds, seals up the sources of illusion. Initially the true pupil of the spirit will acquire sufficient preparatory knowledge about all that might cause illusion and self-deception, so that he can safeguard himself against these. More than anyone he will have the opportunity to become objective in his judgement of life. Everything he learns will keep him from harbouring vague inklings and suggestions, for his schooling makes him as careful and particular as possible. In addition, every true schooling initially leads us to form an idea of great world phenomena, and thus things that require us to use our power of judgement in a way that refines and hones it. Only if someone were to reject the idea of exploring such distant realms, instead focusing only on 'revelations' closer to home, might he then lose the acuity of healthy powers of judgement that give him assurance in distinguishing between illusion and reality. Yet the most important thing of all lies in the exercises themselves that are used in pursuing a correct mode of spiritual schooling. During inner contemplation these must enable the pupil's awareness to survey all that is occurring in the soul. To engender the imaginative faculty a symbol is first created that still contains outer perceptions in pictorial form. Thus its content is not solely determined by him: he does not create it himself. He can therefore be deceived about how it arises, wrongly interpreting its origins. But when he rises to exercises concerned with the faculty of Inspiration, the pupil removes this content from his awareness, immersing himself instead only in his own activity of soul. There too error is still possible. Through education, learning, etc. we acquire our characteristic mode of soul activity. We cannot know everything about its origins. Yet now the pupil of the spirit also removes this soul activity of his from his consciousness. If anything at all remains at this point, there is *nothing* intrinsic to it that we cannot survey. Nothing can adulterate it that we cannot evaluate in relation to its whole content. Thus, in his Intuition the spiritual pupil has something that shows him the clear and distinct nature of the reality of the world of soul and spirit. By measuring anything that comes into his field of observation against these clearly known characteristics of soul-spiritual reality he can distinguish appearance from reality. And he can be sure that invoking this lawfulness will protect him from illusion in the supersensible world in the same way that, in the world of physical reality, he will not confuse an imagined piece of red-hot iron with one that actually burns him. It is self-evident that this applies only to the insights gained from one's own experiences in supersensible worlds and not to those one receives as communications from others, which we grasp with our physical power of reason and our healthy sense of truth. The spiritual pupil will endeavour to make a clear distinction between insight he has acquired either in the former or the latter way. On the one hand he will willingly attend to accounts of higher worlds and seek to grasp them through his power of judgement. But when he refers to something in his own experience, something he has himself observed, he will have carefully tested whether this has impressed itself on him without any illusion, with the qualities he has learned to ascribe to true Intuitions.

After encountering the Guardian of the Threshold, the pupil of the spirit will meet with further experiences as he ascends into supersensible worlds. First of all he will notice the inner affinity between this Guardian and the soul faculty that appeared as the seventh in the account above [p. 16] and took the form of an independent entity. Indeed, this seventh entity is in a sense nothing other than the Guardian of the Threshold himself. And it confronts the spiritual pupil with a particular task. He must guide and direct what his ordinary self contains, and what appears as image before him, through his newborn self. A kind of battle with the double commences, and the latter will continually try to gain the upper hand. To develop the right relationship to this double, not allowing him to do anything that is not governed by the newborn I, strengthens and stabilizes our powers.

In the higher world, self-knowledge is in fact different in nature from what it is in the physical world of the senses. Whereas self-knowledge arises only as inner experience in the latter realm, the newborn self immediately appears as an external soul phenomenon. We see our newborn self before us like another being, but we cannot fully perceive it. This is because, however far we may have come in our journey into higher worlds, higher levels always await us. As we advance we will perceive ever more of this 'higher self', which at any particular stage can always only partially reveal itself. But there is an enormous temptation that arises when we first become partially aware of this 'higher self': to regard it, in a sense, from the point of view we have become accustomed to in the physical world. In fact this is a *good* temptation, and inevitably arises if our development is to proceed in the right way. We have to observe what arises in us as double, as Guardian of the Threshold, and place it before the 'higher self' so that we perceive the gap that still exists between what we are and what we should become. As we do so, though, the

Guardian of the Threshold begins to assume a quite different form, appearing now as an image of all the *hindrances* obstructing the development of the higher self. Here we will see what a burden hampers our ordinary self. And if our preparations have not strengthened us sufficiently to say, 'I will not stop here, but tirelessly develop and advance towards the higher self,' we will weaken and draw back in alarm from what faces us. Though we have dipped into the soul-spiritual world we lose the will to work our way forward through it. Then we become imprisoned by the figure that stands before our soul as the Guardian of the Threshold. But the significant thing here is that we do not have the feeling of being imprisoned, and will believe we are experiencing something quite different. The figure who invokes the Guardian of the Threshold can induce in the soul of the observer an impression that, in the pictures which arise at this stage of development, he already has before him the whole scope of all possible worlds, and that he stands at the summit of knowledge and has no further need to exert himself. Instead of feeling oneself to be a prisoner, one can believe oneself to be the immeasurably rich possessor of all cosmic secrets. That such an experience—the very opposite of the true state of affairs—is possible will not surprise anyone who realizes that it unfolds in the world of soul and spirit, in which events can characteristically appear as the reverse of their actual nature. [...]

The figure we perceive at this stage of development shows us something other than the one that first appeared to us as the Guardian of the Threshold. This double showed us all the qualities intrinsic to the human being's ordinary self, resulting from the influence of Lucifer. But in the course of human evolution the influence of Lucifer made it possible for another power to enter the human soul. This is [...] the power of Ahriman [...] which prevents us as human beings in physical, sensory existence from perceiving the soul-spiritual beings behind the veil of sensory things. The figure who now appears in the experience I have described reveals what the human soul has become under the influence of this second power. If we are properly prepared for this experience, it will show us its true interpretation; and then another figure will soon appear—which we can call the 'Greater Guardian of the Threshold' as distinct from the 'Lesser Guardian'—who tells the pupil that he must not stand still at this stage but must continue to work energetically. He invokes in the observer an awareness that the world he has so far mastered can only become truth, rather than lapse into illusion, if he continues to work in the right way. But if unprepared due to the wrong kind of spiritual schooling, this experience of encountering the Greater Guardian of the Threshold would pour into our soul something that can only be compared with a feeling of immeasurable terror and boundless fear.

The encounter with the Lesser Guardian enables the pupil to test whether he is safe from illusions caused by projecting his own being upon the supersensible world, whereas the experiences that ultimately lead to the Greater Guardian allow him to discover whether he can combat the illusions we ascribed to the second source of error. If he can resist the huge illusion that the world of pictures he has come to perceive is a rich possession, whereas in reality he is imprisoned there, he will be safe from taking appearance as reality in the further course of his development.

To a certain extent the Guardian of the Threshold will assume a different form for each individual. The encounter with him, in fact, corresponds to the experience that allows us to overcome the personal character of our supersensible observations and makes it possible for us to enter a region of experience that is uncoloured by personal predilection, and holds true for every human being.

2. Seeking to Form an Idea of the 'Guardian of the Threshold'

When the soul achieves the capacity to observe something other than through the body's senses, certain difficulties can arise in the life of feelings. The psyche can find itself compelled to adopt a quite different stance towards itself than it was previously accustomed to. Previously it related to the sensory world as a surrounding, external world, in contrast to the inner possession of its experiences. It cannot relate to the external supersensible world in the same way. As soon as it perceives this external world, you can say that it flows into and merges with it; it cannot consider itself separate from it in the same way that it regards the external world of the senses. In consequence, everything it considers its own inner world in this supersensible environment assumes a distinct character that is initially hard to reconcile with ideas of interior life. You can no longer say, 'I think, I feel or I have my thoughts and I shape them.' Instead you have to say, 'Something thinks in me, allows feelings to light up in me; something shapes my thoughts so that they surface in a very particular way and reveal their presence in my awareness.'

This sense of things can have an extremely oppressive quality when it becomes clear that our mode of supersensible experience does indeed give us a true experience of reality and that we are not just succumbing to fantasy or illusion. We discover that the supersensible environment wishes to feel and think itself in us, but that it is prevented from producing what it desires. At the same time we gain a sense that what wishes to enter our soul is true reality, and that it alone is able to clarify for us what we have previously experienced as reality. This feeling also assumes the form of showing supersensible reality as something that is infinitely more radiant in worth compared to the reality which the soul has known hitherto. The oppressive quality is due to our realization that the next step we must take must be willed. Taking this step lies in the essential nature of what we have become through our inner experience. If we were not to take it, this would be like a denial of what we are, an act of self-destruction even. And yet at the same time this can be accompanied by the feeling that we are powerless to do it, or that it will remain imperfect however well we attempt it.

All this transforms into the idea that the soul, by its intrinsic nature, faces a task that it cannot accomplish because this nature is not accepted by the supersensible environment, which does not wish to incorporate it. Thus the soul comes to feel itself at odds with the supersensible world; it has to acknowledge that its own nature is not such that it can merge with this world. Yet only this world can reveal true reality to it, and show the psyche how it relates to this true reality. In other words, the soul feels it has sundered itself from a capacity to properly observe the truth. This feeling signifies an experience which becomes increasingly decisive for the whole worth of our soul. We feel ourselves, with our whole life, to be rooted in an error. Yet this error is different from others, which are errors of thought whereas this one is direct experience. An error of thought can be remedied by replacing an erroneous idea with a correct one. This *exis-*

tential error, by contrast, has become a part of the very life of our psyche. We ourselves are this error; we cannot simply improve it for it exists, is part of reality and indeed of our own reality, however we may think about it. Such an experience is devastating for our own self. We feel our interior life to be painfully rejected by everything we long for. This pain, which we experience at a certain stage of our soul's pilgrimage, far exceeds any pain we might experience in the sense world; and therefore it can exceed everything we have become capable of surmounting through the inner life we have hitherto known. It can have a paralysing effect. The soul fearfully asks where it can find the powers to endure the task that faces it. It has to find these powers within its own life, and they consist in what we can regard as inner courage, as inner fearlessness.

To progress further in the soul's pilgrimage we must learn to draw these powers of endurance from within, accessing the inner courage and inner fearlessness we would not normally need when we live through our body's senses. Such powers only arise through true self-knowledge. It is really only at this stage of development that we discover how little we really knew about ourselves before. We have been used to relying on our inner sense of things, without regarding this as one regards a part of the external environment. But through the steps that lead to a developing capacity to experience things outside the body, we acquire a particular means of self-knowledge. In a sense we learn to regard ourselves from a perspective that only arises when we are outside the body. And the oppressive feeling I have described is itself the beginning of true self-knowledge. To experience ourselves in error in our relationship to the external world in fact reveals the real nature of our own being of soul to us.

Now it lies in the nature of the human soul to experience such insight into itself as painful. Only when we feel this pain do we discover how strong is the very natural longing to regard oneself as a very significant person. This trait may seem most unattractive, but we have to freely face up to the unattractive nature of our own self. We have not previously felt it because we have never really penetrated our own being consciously before. Only at such a moment can we discover that we love in ourselves what we ought really to find ugly: we become aware of the full scope of our self-love. And at the same time we find how little inclination we have to divest ourselves of this self-love. When we are concerned with qualities of the soul involved in ordinary life, in our relationships with others, the difficulties are already great enough. Through true self-knowledge, for example, we may find that a person to whom we thought we were well inclined in fact evokes in the depths of our soul a hidden envy or hatred or suchlike. We discover that these feelings that have not yet surfaced will quite certainly come to expression at some point; and that it would be very superficial to think that because we have recognized these feelings we can tell ourselves to eradicate such envy or hatred. Instead we find that such a thought will be very weak, will make very little headway, when the urge to express this hatred or envy breaks forth from the soul with something like elemental power. Self-knowledge of this kind will arise in one or another person depending on the nature of his soul, surfacing when sense-free experience occurs—since then self-knowledge will be true, no longer obscured by the wish to see oneself in some way in a favourable light.

These kinds of self-knowledge are painful, and oppressive for the soul, but unavoidable for anyone who wishes to acquire the ability to experience things outside of the body. They arise necessarily as a result of the whole distinctive relationship which we must adopt towards our own soul. It requires the strongest powers of soul to engage in quite general, human self-knowledge. We have to observe ourselves from a perspective lying outside of our previous soul experience. We have to say this to ourselves: 'Hitherto you have observed and judged things and processes in the world in a way that simply lies in your human nature. But now try to imagine you are unable to observe and evaluate them in this way—then you would not be what you are, and would have no inner experience of these things. You yourself would be nothing.' It is necessary not only for an ordinary person to say this to himself, someone who only rarely formulates thoughts and questions about the world and about life, but also every scientist and philosopher. You see, philosophy too is only a way of observing and evaluating the world in accordance with human soul life but cannot be reconciled with the supersensible environment. The latter repulses it. In fact, everything is repulsed that we have so far been. We look back upon our whole soul, on our I, as something of which we must divest ourselves if we wish to enter the supersensible world. The soul is unable to regard this I as anything other than its real being before it enters the supersensible world. It inevitably regards it as its true human nature. It has to say, this I of mine is what I need to form ideas about the world; I must not relinquish this I for otherwise I will be lost. The soul contains the strongest urge to sustain and preserve this I so as not to lose the solid ground beneath it. But what the soul inevitably finds justified in ordinary life is something it may no longer feel as soon as it enters the supersensible environment. Here it crosses a threshold where it must not only leave one or another prized possession behind, but above all the strength of its greatest truth must appear here as the greatest error.

The soul can draw back in alarm from such a requirement. Fulfilling this can appear too great a surrender, can be felt as a kind of annihilation of its own being so great that at this threshold it acknowledges its inability to satisfy this demand. Such an admission can assume all kinds of different forms: it can arise instinctively and appear in a quite different guise from its real nature to a person thinking and acting in accordance with it. Such a person, for example, may feel a deep aversion towards all supersensible truths, regarding them as fantasy and reverie. He only sees things in this way because in depths of soul he is unaware of, he is secretly afraid of these truths. He has a feeling that he can only live with what his senses and rational judgement show him, and therefore he avoids approaching the threshold of the supersensible world. But he veils this avoidance in the guise of something he regards as untenable when measured against the yardstick of reason and science. In fact he loves reason and science in the form he knows them because they are bound up with his I. This is a very common form of self-love, but one that cannot go with us as we cross the threshold into the supersensible world.

Such instinctive withdrawal from the threshold is not

however the only possible form of holding back. Someone may approach it consciously but then turn round again as it were, because he fears what awaits him. In this case he will not easily erase the effects that arise in his ordinary soul as he approaches the threshold, which will result in the experience of incapacity spreading out over his whole life of soul.

What we need to do is develop the ability to divest ourselves, when we enter the supersensible world, of what we experience in ordinary life as our most potent truth, and instead adapt to a different way of being, of experiencing things and evaluating them. It is important to be clear that we must certainly make use of ways of feeling and judging the world that hold good in relation to the sense world. We have to learn not only to live in two different worlds, but to live in each in a quite different way. Because we have to judge differently in another world does not mean that we allow our healthy judgement to be impaired in ordinary life, in the rational world of the senses.

Adopting this stance is difficult for people. We acquire the capacity for it only by persevering, by energetically and patiently strengthening our life of soul. In experiencing the threshold, we can feel that *not* to be led to it is a boon for our ordinary sensibility. The feelings that arise in us inevitably give us the sense that this boon derives from a living power that protects human beings from the danger of experiencing the terrors of self-annihilation at the threshold. Behind the outer world we know as a given in ordinary life stands another. Before its threshold stands a strict guardian who ensures [initially] that a person learn nothing of the laws of the supersensible world. You see, all uncertainty about this world is easier to endure than vision of what one must leave behind in order to cross its threshold.

A person will remain protected from such experiences as long as he does not approach the threshold himself. Listening to accounts of these experiences from those who have come to or crossed it does not lessen such protection. In fact, such accounts will positively aid someone when he does approach the threshold. In this case, as in many others, it is true to say that we accomplish something better if we have previously already formed some idea of what it involves. Such prior knowledge however does not replace the self-knowledge that we need to journey into the supersensible world. But it is incorrect to say, as some clairvoyant people do, or those familiar with the nature of clairvoyance, that these matters should never be spoken of amongst people who have not actually resolved to enter the supersensible world themselves. We live at a time when people increasingly need to become aware of the nature of the supersensible world if they are to cope inwardly with life's challenges. Publicizing spiritual insights, including those relating to the Guardian of the Threshold, is a task intrinsic to our work both now and in the near future.

3. The Guardian of the Threshold and Some Characteristics of Supersensible Consciousness

Living in the world of the senses, we stand outside the world of spirit in which [. . .] our being is rooted. We see the effect on our nature of this ordinary experience if we consider that supersensible consciousness, which enters supersensible worlds, requires us to strengthen the powers of soul acquired in the sense world. Without strengthening these capacities, the soul will feel a certain timidity about entering the world of spirit. It will even defend itself against experiencing this world by seeking 'proofs' that such experience is impossible.

But if it finds itself strong enough to enter the supersensible world, the psyche will perceive within itself the powers that allow it to maintain its autonomy when doing so, experiencing in its awareness not only thoughts but also entities—as it inevitably must in the elemental and spiritual world. At the same time it will discover that it has only been able to gather these powers during life in the sense world; and it recognizes the necessity of passing through the sense world in its cosmic journey.

In particular, this insight arises through experiences which supersensible consciousness has in relation to *thinking*. When it enters the elemental world, consciousness is filled with beings perceived in the form of pictures. It is quite unable to engage with the beings of this world with an inner soul activity reminiscent of thinking in the sense world. And yet it would be impossible to find one's way through this elemental world without using the power of thought. Without thinking observation we would *see* the beings of the elemental world but would be unable to discern their true nature. It would be like having a text before us in a script we cannot decipher, which we can see just like anyone else but cannot read. Only someone who knows the script can find meaning and reality in it.

While dwelling in the elemental world, however, super-sensible awareness in no way activates thinking in the same way as we do in the sense world. Instead we can say that a thinking being—such as the human being—implicitly perceives the meaning of the beings and powers of the elemental worlds through proper vision of this world, whereas a non-thinking being would perceive the pictures there without any sense of their meaning or reality.

On entering the world of spirit, we would for example think the ahrimanic beings to be quite different in nature from what they are if our soul, as thinking entity, did not perceive them. The same is true of luciferic and other beings of the spiritual world. The ahrimanic and luciferic beings are seen by us in their reality when we view them from the world of spirit with a clairvoyant gaze that has been strengthened by thinking.

If the soul did not arm itself with adequate thinking power, then the luciferic beings perceived from the world of spirit would usurp the clairvoyant world of pictures, invoking in the soul of the observer the illusion that it is penetrating ever deeper into the spiritual world it seeks. In reality, though, this soul will be submerging itself increasingly in the world the luciferic beings wish to concoct as one identical with their nature. The soul would feel itself to be ever more autonomous but would in fact be entering ever further into a world of spirit that does not correspond to its actual nature and deeper origins. It would arrive in a spiritual environment alien to it.

The sense world hides all view of such entities as the luciferic, and within this world, therefore, they are unable to confuse or mislead our awareness. They are simply not present for us there. And our awareness can therefore sufficiently strengthen its thinking powers without disturbance from these entities. One of the instinctive characteristics of healthy consciousness is that it only wishes to enter the world of spirit to the extent that, in the sense world, it has strengthened itself sufficiently to orientate itself in supersensible realms. Consciousness clings to the way in which it can experience itself within the world of senses. There it feels itself in its element, experiencing itself in thoughts, feelings and affects, etc. that it owes to the sensory world.

We can see how determinedly our awareness clings to these experiences the moment we really enter worlds of spirit. In the same way that we cling to fond memories at certain moments of our life, so at the moment we enter supersensible worlds all the appetites we are capable of necessarily arise from our depths of soul; we become aware how we rely fundamentally on the life that connects us with the sensory world. This dependency appears here in its full reality, without any of the illusions we otherwise form about it during life. As we enter the world of spirit, an aspect of self-knowledge comes about—as our first supersensible achievement—of which previously we can have had scarcely any inkling. And we discover all that we must leave behind if we really wish to enter with full knowledge into the world in which we are actually always immersed. There rises before the inner gaze a very sharp and clear awareness of what we have so far made of ourselves as human beings, both consciously and unconsciously, in the sensory world.

This experience can often lead to a person relinquishing all further attempts to penetrate supersensible worlds. You see, one gains insight into how one must learn to feel and sense things differently if the sojourn in worlds of spirit is to be successful. One has to resolve to develop a quite different inner condition of soul than one previously had. Or, to put it differently, we have to complement what we have so far achieved with something new.

And yet, what actually happens at such a moment, when we step over the threshold of the supersensible world? We perceive the being that we have always been, yet not now from the sense world which was always previously the realm we viewed everything from. No, we perceive it *without illusion*, in its truth and reality, from the world of spirit. Perceiving this, we feel fully imbued with the powers of knowledge which, in the world of spirit, are capable of evaluating it. In observing ourselves in this way we also discover why no one can desire to enter the supersensible world consciously without great reticence; we perceive the degree of strength that we possess for penetrating this realm. We see how we hold ourselves at a distance from it. And the more clearly we see through ourselves, the stronger do we discover the inclinations by means of which we desire to preserve our awareness in the sense world. Our enhanced knowledge draws these inclinations up into visibility for us from the hidden corners of the soul. *We have to recognize them,* for that is the only way to overcome them. But as we recognize and perceive them they bring intensified proof of their strength. They wish to master the soul, which feels itself to be drawn down by them into obscure depths. This moment of self-knowledge is an earnest one. The word 'self-knowledge' is bandied about too much in philosophical discourses and theories; and, rather than nurturing it, this actually diverts people's gaze from the seriousness connected with it. Yet despite the gravity of these things, we can feel gratified to think that human nature is restrained by its instincts from entering the world of spirit before it is able to develop the necessary maturity in its self-observation and experience. How absolutely right it is that our first, highly significant encounter with a being of the supersensible world is with our own being in its full reality—which we are called upon to develop further in the course of human evolution.

We can say that a being lies within us who carefully guards the boundary that must be crossed when we enter the supersensible world. This spiritual being within us—who is us ourselves—whom we can however perceive as little with ordinary consciousness as the eye can perceive itself, is the Guardian of the Threshold in the world of spirit. We learn to perceive him the moment we not only are him in reality but, standing outside him, see him *as if he were another.*

Like other experiences of supersensible worlds, the faculties of soul we have intensified and inwardly strengthened also render the Guardian of the Threshold visible. You see, apart from the fact that our encounter with the 'Guardian' is raised to the level of conscious knowledge for the clairvoyant gaze, this encounter is not an event that only occurs for a person who has developed the capacity for spiritual vision. The very same circumstances that constitute this encounter arise for everyone whenever they fall asleep, and for as long as sleep lasts we stand outside ourselves in a way that is identical with standing before the Guardian of the Threshold. During sleep the soul raises itself to its supersensible being. But its inner powers are as yet not strong enough to awaken awareness of itself.

It is also of particular importance for understanding supersensible experience, especially in its subtle beginnings, to be aware that the soul may already have begun to experience supersensibly without as yet being able to form any particular notion of this. Clairvoyance begins in a very delicate way—and in the expectation of perceiving something almost tangible, we may often fail to notice very fleeting clairvoyant impressions or may not wish to acknowledge them as such. They arise in a way that already invites them to be forgotten, entering our field of awareness so faintly that they remain wholly disregarded, like wisps of soul cloud. Because of this, and because people usually expect spiritual vision to be quite different from what it is, earnest seekers of a world of spirit often do not find it. In this respect, too, the encounter with the Guardian of the Threshold is important. Having strengthened the soul specifically in relation to self-knowledge, this encounter itself may only be like a first, subtle and fleeting glimpse of spiritual vision. Nevertheless, we are unlikely to let it be forgotten so easily as other supersensible impressions since we are more interested in our own being than in other things. It is not essential, however, that the encounter with the Guardian be among our first supersensible experiences. The soul can strengthen in various directions. Before this encounter with the Guardian the soul may go in directions in which other beings or phenomena enter its field of spiritual vision. But it is true to say that this encounter will occur relatively soon after we enter the supersensible world.

4. Morality on the Path of Knowledge

Today let us start with a well-known requirement for all who wish to progress not only in knowledge of spiritual science but also, perhaps, in their inner development. It has been emphasized time and again that a person's purity of aims and loving intentions are vital for his inner development, leading possibly to his own experiences in the world of spirit. It might be one-sided to say this (though everything one says is inevitably one-sided), but a spiritual researcher or anyone at all who wishes to ascend into worlds of spirit requires a particular quality of soul: that of sympathizing, and doing so energetically, with what is good, noble, beautiful; and of feeling aversion, in a sense, for what is evil or ugly.

The moral purity of our soul nature is called for continually when we pursue a path into worlds of spirit. To do this in a way that fully accords with the nature of our times, our soul must be completely imbued with true, moral aims and intentions. Later we will hear that it is possible, however, to develop clairvoyant powers without meeting these basic conditions; yet failing to do so will always have a somewhat dubious character.

To understand why this is so, let us first explore what we mean by morality in human nature. On the one hand we find it necessary to speak of human morality when we consider the drives and urges of external necessity impelling us to act, will or desire. Whenever we are impelled to wish, will or act in some way to meet our natural needs such as hunger or thirst, we do not of course think that such wishing or will leads to moral action. This does not of course mean that they have to be immoral either. But when a stone falls to the ground, this involves no moral action, and we see no reason whatever to apply standards of morality to it. Just as little do we invoke morality when a person satisfies the natural requirements of his organism when eating or drinking. Nor do we feel it necessary to speak of morality if someone sees a beautiful flower somewhere, or some other beautiful object and, because it strikes him as pleasing and beautiful, is motivated to desire or possess it. Here too we leave morality out of the picture.

So when do we find morality in human nature? Surely only when we do something that is not impelled by external necessities, such as hunger or thirst, or the pleasure that an object awakens in us, but instead when we act out of the inmost core of our being. This is like a command arising within us that is quite independent of any outward cause. We can be especially aware of the difference between this moral sphere and, not immorality, but let us say a morally indifferent domain, when we consider the possibility of refraining from doing something or other impelled by outer circumstances because we hearken to an inner command in us not to do it.

Let's take a fairly familiar, if trivial example. Someone has a strong inclination to drink a great deal. If he is able to do so, he drinks. Or, equally, he can hearken to an inner voice that has nothing to do with this inclination itself but opposes this outward urge, and says: 'Do not do what you feel impelled to!' Here we find something speaking in us that contradicts the outward cause. We regard all such inner opposition to and censuring of our own actions as moral. And so we can only speak of moral actions if we disregard all external impressions, all that compels us outwardly, and hearken to what speaks from within us. It is this, after all, that raises us above the animals: that we can hear within us a voice above and beyond the urge of outer causation, one capable of resisting or opposing the latter.

We inevitably feel that there is something intrinsically true in the moral domain. Such intrinsic truth is the primary characteristic of all moral impulses, one which outward circumstances cannot impinge on when we judge an action to be moral or immoral. If we refer to something as moral that seemingly occurs through an outward cause, this is usually illusory. It would be an illusion to find morality in external dictates. For instance, it is not a moral deed if we eat in adherence to the principle that is necessary to survive as physical organism, rather than just satisfying hunger and thirst. Morality arises only when we complement an outer with an inner impulse. It is right and good for people to sustain themselves on earth, not just to fulfil their outward tasks but the inner ones which follow from them, and here morality does enter into the picture. Otherwise we have only the appearance of morality. Real morality is distinguished by an impulse not caused by the external world, but arising purely from the springs of our own soul.

Now of course someone might say that there are also wicked voices within us: we frequently hearken to impulses that we recognize clearly as inner ones but are anything other than moral. Here we can say [...] that whenever someone hearkens to these apparently inner impulses, which are immoral or evil, he is in fact not hearkening to his own deeper self but to impulses whose origin he is unaware of, which he confuses with those that arise within. Our spiritual-scientific observations have taught us about luciferic powers: these come not from within but in a sense approach us from without, since luciferic entities have taken up residence in our astral body, not in our I. You see, whenever we try to define morality we come up against numerous contradictions.

If we go into this more carefully we discover that morality is characterized by impulses arising from the inmost core of our being. Here—residing entirely in our inner, intrinsic self—what we find morally agreeable, what invokes our moral pleasure and can fill us with delight and enthusiasm, can become our ideal. In ordinary life already, it is of very great benefit, is very necessary, for us to realize that we are only fully rooted in ourselves in moral judgements or judgements that arise in a similar way; and for practical esotericism this is an absolute requirement, and must be acknowledged as a founding esoteric principle. For the esoteric pupil everything that happens in him must be governed by a moral impulse, so that nothing occurs in the soul as one embarks upon a path of higher knowledge that is not in full accord with truly moral impulses.

Someone who wishes to become a practical esotericist and pursue the path of knowledge must not undertake or carry out anything of which he cannot say that it closely resembles the moral nature he finds within him. At no point may the path of knowledge diverge from conduct that is in close affinity with moral impulses. The path of knowledge has a close affinity with morality, even down to small details, and I would like to clarify this with a specific example.

Morality in modern human beings has a very distinctive character. You can say that the Ten Commandments are still, after all, the most important laws governing human conduct. If we examine them in more detail we find they assume a distinct form. Of the ten, only a few state that 'Thou shalt . . .' do something, while the other seven state 'Thou shalt *not* . . .' Thus cosmic powers, we discover, regard it as much more necessary to give humankind moral imperatives telling us *not* to do than to do something. In general therefore, morality has to work in human nature in a way predicated on saying 'Thou shalt not . . .'

Let's take a closer look still at this aspect of the Ten Commandments. Those—the majority—that tell us 'Thou shalt not . . .' all relate to external things, to what we ought not to do in the physical world. The couple of others, by contrast, which say 'Thou shalt . . .' relate really to what exceeds the bounds of the physical world: 'Thou shalt have no other gods before me,'* 'Remember the Sabbath day, to keep it holy.' Here we see that matters primarily spiritual in nature are referred to in positive terms whereas all the commandments that focus on moral conduct in external life are couched in terms of *not* doing something. Even if the fourth commandment—'Honour thy father and mother that

---

* Translator's note: In the King James version this is couched negatively, whereas in the German the words literally are: 'Thou shalt believe in one God.'

thy days may be long upon the land which the Lord thy God giveth thee'—appears to be positive, we can sense that it also has a strongly negative character like most of the others. This is a kind of transitional commandment which, while relating to the physical world, already begins to lead us away from it into the world of spirit. We can demonstrate this specifically in the fact that all older cultures were based on so-called ancestor worship, of whom one's immediate forefathers are just a special instance: a kind of transition from the sense world to the higher world. However, this fourth commandment relates especially to the immediate physical world and the relationship between parents and children. We can fulfil it in relation to our parents, can feel that the fourth commandment is initially couched in positive terms but that it has been established, nevertheless, to *prevent* something happening. By contrast the first commandments relate to realities that are not present at all in the physical world.

The way these ten commandments are structured points us to a key characteristic of morality in the sensory world: that our moral impulses contradict what we would do if we merely followed the urges and drives of the physical world. For the path of knowledge, governed as it must be by moral impulses and having close affinity with them, this means no less than that we moralize all our perception and knowledge: laws of knowledge that are otherwise merely theoretical must here become inner moral laws. Thus when we observe with inner knowledge the immediate physical plane that spreads around us, it must be extinguished. We extinguish it in the same way that our lower appetites are extinguished when the moral exhortation of 'Thou shalt not' resounds.

This is why every genuine account of the path of knowledge accentuates the fact that we raise ourselves most surely into the higher world by enhancing our moral impulses. This comes to expression in the tiniest details. Let us imagine a plant for instance. What external impulse do we initially find proceeding from it? Take the leaf of the plant. The external impulse we find here is that the leaves appear green to us. In the physical, sensory world, rose leaves, for instance, are green. But as a practical esotericist—someone who really seeks higher knowledge, which forms in accordance with moral insights—one would regard this leaf and find the inner impulse, 'You shall not be green' awakening in response to it. It must be possible for us to observe the green leaf with a power of vision that cancels the external impulse; and that just as a bad tendency is extinguished before our moral judgement, the greenness of the leaf likewise is extinguished through another—let us call it clairvoyant—power.

Indeed, when someone develops his clairvoyant powers in the right way, as described in *Knowledge of the Higher Worlds*, he can observe the green leaf and, in the same way that moral judgements extinguish bad tendencies, extinguish the green quality of the leaf which holds true only in the physical plane. And where green otherwise appears, clairvoyant vision in this case perceives something resembling a light reddish or peach-blossom colour. This appears when we can cancel what exists on the physical plane through our clairvoyant faculty and draw out the supersensible quality that underlies sensory things. Embarking on the path of knowledge, therefore, can really be seen as occurring in the same way as a person's moral experience. The action of the supersensible on the sensory world does really occur in the same way that a moral impulse works upon immoral tendencies. If we observe the rose itself, on the other hand—this rose here, say, which has such a full-bodied red on the physical plane—we would see this rose as a brightly shining, diaphanous green, and for the paler rose here a kind of dense green with a somewhat bluish tinge.

This is just one instance where we discover that soul qualities in esoteric judgements formed through clairvoyant vision are composed in the same way that moral judgements extinguish what is immoral. This substantiates what we said at the beginning: in order to come to higher knowledge we have to learn to extinguish the immediate impressions we receive from the external, physical world—to make *maya* vanish so that something else can replace it.

It is well known that the easiest way to learn a skill is to practise related skills, things that resemble or have an affinity with it. No one tries to learn something by preoccupying himself with quite different things. As far as I know, no one becomes a mathematician by going for a walk, simply because the two activities have nothing in common. In the same way, soul faculties that resemble moral impulses can only be acquired by practising things we already possess in ordinary life. While we may not yet have clairvoyant vision, which takes long and arduous effort, we always have the opportunity to contemplate and ponder what it is we consider to be morally good or morally indefensible.

Most people, after all, do not fail to act morally because they do not know what morality is, but only because their appetites, urges, desires or passions contradict their moral insight. Having studied ourselves carefully we can then return to something within us that affirms what we may call morality. And in our meditation we can ask ourselves how our moral judgement can think of a particular aspect of the world. We can form inner images and contemplate these and, in doing so, we will experience certain things and habits of feeling in our soul—they will really mature within us— which are related to powers of clairvoyance.

In other words, the first thing one can do to awaken clairvoyant powers is to reconcile our moral thinking with our actions. This is the best way to school clairvoyant powers; and this is why we always emphasize that clairvoyant powers should really only be achieved by enhancing our moral character.

But in thinking about this we will have to ask whether other means exist to develop clairvoyant vision. People whose conduct does not strike us as moral in the least often arrive at high levels of clairvoyant ability; and we cannot assume therefore that they have first schooled their conduct, their pleasure and displeasure, their enthusiasm, by nurturing the power of moral judgement. We discover that people who have developed clairvoyant capacities by all kinds of other means reveal various negative qualities that they used not to have, or scarcely had. They may for instance turn into out-and-out liars when they start to develop clairvoyance. In fact, it can sometimes be very dangerous for a person's character if, in particular, he becomes clairaudient. How can this be reconciled with what was said a moment ago? The path of knowledge should be governed by aspects I have described today, and I made this point in various key passages in my book *Knowledge of the Higher Worlds*; yet there are certainly other paths. Studying the path of knowledge in the right way we will soon discover why negative qualities can arise. We bear within us our soul-spiritual core whose essence we encapsulate whenever we say 'I' or 'I am'. This soul-spiritual core of our being is embedded in the astral, ether and physical body. The way we live today in the world is, inwardly, really within our I, for in waking life all the faculties of our soul are in some way connected with the I, and as it were appear against this background.

5. Self-knowledge and Nearness to Christ

Without actually describing the Rosicrucian path today, we will explore the essential character both of this path and of the modern path of knowledge. In the abstract we can say these paths are distinguished by the fact that anyone who gives advice and guidance on initiation retains a profound respect for the autonomy and inviolability of the human will sphere. The following is therefore a key aspect: the ordinary, natural configuration of physical body, etheric body, astral body and I is changed here by cultivating morality and spirituality in a very particular way. Guidance in cultivating moral sensibility as well as concentration of thinking, meditation, ultimately focuses on loosening the spiritual framework connecting the human etheric and physical bodies. This results in our etheric body no longer being so strongly embedded and incorporated in the physical body as it is naturally predisposed to be.

All exercises aim to bring about this loosening and lifting of the etheric body, which at the same time, however, causes a different kind of connection to develop between the astral and etheric bodies. In ordinary life the etheric and physical bodies are, to a great extent, firmly connected, and this means that our astral body is unable to sense or experience everything that occurs in its etheric body. While the etheric body is anchored in the physical body, our astral body and I only perceive what the physical body imparts to them and what it enables them to think through the instrument of the brain. The etheric body is too deeply implanted in the physical body in ordinary life for us to feel it to be an autonomous entity, an autonomous tool of perception and also a tool of feeling and will.

Our efforts in concentrated thinking, guidance for which will be given today, as the Rosicrucians also gave it—our meditative labours and the cleansing of moral feelings—all ultimately render the etheric body autonomous in a way described in *Knowledge of the Higher Worlds.* In the same way that we use our eyes to see and our hands to grasp things, we can begin to use the etheric body with its organs to look into the world of spirit rather than the physical world. The way in which we take hold of our inner life and focus it inwardly works to make the etheric body independent.

Yet this cannot be done without first, at least tentatively, imbuing ourselves with the idea of practical karma. In practice we can do this by establishing a certain moral equilibrium, a certain balance in our powers of feeling. Anyone who cannot make any headway with the idea that we are all, ultimately, responsible for our drives and inclinations will not get very far. A certain equanimity and insight—even if this is only hypothetical insight into karma—is the necessary point of departure. Someone who cannot detach himself from his ego and clings to his narrow mode of feeling, his limited sensibility, in such a way that he repeatedly blames others rather than himself when things go wrong, and who continually feels that the world or those around him are against him and therefore, in a sense, to put it rather trivially, is a grumbler who cannot get beyond a self-centred view of the world—one we do get beyond in ordinary thinking and can learn from exoteric theosophy [anthroposophy]—will find it extremely difficult indeed to make any progress.

It is therefore a good idea to develop inner equanimity and composure by recognizing that if we do not succeed in doing something, on an esoteric path especially, we can only blame ourselves. This is the best way to get further. By contrast, we do ourselves least favours here by finding fault with some external aspect, continually switching methods or paths for instance. This is more important than may initially be apparent. Whenever we scrutinize ourselves properly and discover how little progress we have made, we should seek the fault in ourselves. It actually marks considerable progress if we can resolve to seek any fault in ourselves alone. We will find, if we do, that we then make progress not only in less immediate matters but even in aspects of ordinary daily life.

Those who are aware of such things will always testify to the fact that seeking the fault for some failure or other in oneself reveals something that actually makes our daily life easier. We come to terms much better with our surroundings if we can really embrace this idea. It enables us to get over all kinds of morose behaviour, hypochondria, moaning and complaining, and to go more calmly through life. We need to remember that all true initiation of modern times lays the strictest obligation on anyone who guides others to refrain from entering the inmost sanctum of another's soul. Thus, we have to take responsibility ourselves for our inmost soul, and not complain that no one gave us the advice we needed. We may receive the right advice, but things may still not work out if we ourselves do not resolve to act upon it.

This equanimity and composure, once we have chosen to

pursue it—and choosing this should be a matter of earnest resolve—is a solid foundation upon which to develop a practice of meditation in which we give ourselves up to certain thoughts and feelings. And it is an important aspect of Rosicrucian schooling that in all meditations, concentration exercises and so forth we do not come to rely on any kind of mere dogma but draw on universal human realities.

By contrast we can go astray [...] by starting from something we entertain initially only as a purely personal content. How could we be certain of the right content if this could only be demonstrated by esoteric knowledge and were not generally available to start with? Rosicrucian principles require us to start with solidly founded realities. We have to accept that we are not capable in advance of discerning truths if we rely only on external material documents—for instance, the nature of the Golgotha event. You see, we only gain insights as we become familiar with the esoteric path, and cannot assume knowledge of them in advance. For this reason we start with universally human realities, with things whose validity can be demonstrated to every soul.

Of what kind are such things? Look out into the wide world, admiring the light's revelations, the play of sunlight, and feeling what your eye perceives of it—only light's outer veil, its external manifestation or, as Christian esotericism puts it, the glory of the light. And then give yourself up to the thought that something quite other must be hidden behind this external light we perceive with our senses. This is a universal, human experience: to conceive light spreading through universal space, to perceive it and then realize that in this radiant element of light must live something spiritual that weaves its light-veil through space. You can concentrate on this thought, live in it, and then you have something very universally human which needs no dogma to sustain it but arises through a general, universal sense of things.

Or again, you can feel the warmth of nature, sense how spirit lives in the warmth that surges through the world. And then, sensing a certain affinity in our own organism between this warmth and feelings of love, you can concentrate on this thought: on the spiritual nature of warmth, how it lives and pulses through the world. Following which, you can contemplate what we can learn from intuitions given us in modern esoteric teachings, and discuss with people who have some knowledge in this field how to concentrate, meditate on thoughts that are also universal, cosmic ones. Or again, you can practise purifying and ennobling moral feelings, and this will give you an understanding that what we feel in the moral realm is reality. Here we can go beyond the prejudice that our moral feelings are something transient and fleeting, realizing that our actions live on in their moral impact, as moral being and reality. We can learn here to feel responsibility for the way our moral feelings place us into conscious involvement with the world. Basically, all esoteric life focuses on universally human matters such as these.

Today, though, I would like to describe where we arrive when we engage in this way with exercises based on things that arise from our human nature—at least when we surrender to it in astute self-observation. By doing this we loosen the connection between the physical body and the etheric body, thus acquiring knowledge different from the ordinary.

It is as though we give birth to a second human being in us. We are no longer so firmly bound up with the physical body but instead, at the most beautiful moments of life, our ether body and astral body are as if encapsulated in a separate envelope within it, and we can therefore have the experience of being free of the tool of the physical body.

It is this we accomplish by these means. Yet at the same time we are led to perceive the true being and nature of our physical body and recognize what it brings about in us when we are rooted in it. Only when we emerge from it to some degree do we really perceive the whole action and effect of the physical body: like a snake shedding its skin that can then regard this skin from without, whereas otherwise it feels itself one with it. Only in this way, at the first stage of initiation, do we learn to feel free of our physical body, and can therefore perceive it properly. At this moment we inevitably experience very particular feelings which can initially be described as follows.

There are so many different kinds of experience on the path of initiation, and it has not yet been possible to describe them all. In *Knowledge of the Higher Worlds* you will find much about this, but there too a good many things are not included. What we can first experience, and what almost everyone can experience who takes a step towards the path of knowledge from ordinary life, is the following: 'I myself did not form this physical body of mine which I can see here. I certainly did not create it myself, though it has drawn me towards what I have become in this world. If I did not have this physical body, the I which I now regard as my great ideal would not be bound to me. I have only become what I am by receiving my physical body in a form that has been forged in accordance with my being.'

All this initially gives rise to a sense of grievance or bitterness towards the powers of the cosmos that one has become what one is. It is easy to wish not to harbour such a grievance; yet when we stand before the whole sad majesty of what we have become through the way we are connected with our physical body, this is an overwhelming experience and we do indeed feel something akin to rancour, hatred or bitterness towards the powers of the universe because we have developed as we have. To counter this it is important that our esoteric schooling has advanced far enough at this point for us to overcome this bitterness, recognizing from a higher perspective that we, with our whole being, with our individuality that has descended into its different incarnations, are after all responsible for what our physical body has become. If we overcome this bitterness we stand before the feeling that I have often described: 'Now I know that I myself am the one who appears here as the altered form of my physical existence. I myself am this! I only knew nothing of my physical being because it smothered me.'

This is the significant encounter with the Guardian of the Threshold. But if we arrive at this point, experiencing what I have just described through rigorous practice of our exercises, we emerge from a general human state, from the universally human, and perceive ourselves as the result of previous incarnations, seeing how our form has become what it now is. At the same time, though, we also perceive our capacity to experience the most profound pain, and discover how we must work our way beyond this pain in order to overcome our present form of existence. And for anyone sufficiently advanced in this work, who experiences these feelings in their full intensity, who has had vision of the Guardian of the Threshold, an imagination will inevitably arise that he does not conjure arbitrarily himself—as happens in Jesuitism in picturing events in the Bible—but instead he has a vivid experience of what he himself is, resulting from what he has felt through universally human experience. In consequence he becomes acquainted as a matter of course with the image of the ideal, divine human being, who lives as we do in a physical body, but who also feels within this same physical body everything that a physical body can give rise to.

The temptation and picture described in the synoptic Gospels—the temptation in which Christ is led to the mountain and promised all outer realities—of desiring to cling to outward realities, to cling to material things, that is, of stopping with the Guardian of the Threshold and not progressing beyond him, appears to us in the great, ideal picture of Christ Jesus standing on the mountain with the tempter beside him, as a picture we would encounter even if we had never heard of the Gospels. And then we know that the person who wrote this temptation narrative was describing his own experience: seeing, in the spirit, Christ Jesus and the tempter. And so we know it to be true, true in the spirit, that the Gospel writer described something which we ourselves can experience even if we knew nothing of the Gospels.

We are led to a picture therefore that is identical with that in the Gospels; and here we make what is written there our own possession. No force is brought to bear but instead this is drawn out of the depths of our own nature. Starting from generally human experience our esoteric life gives new birth in us to the Gospels, so that we feel one with the Evangelists. Here another feeling dawns in us, as a next stage in a sense of the esoteric path. We feel how the tempter who has appeared here expands into a mighty being standing behind all the world's phenomena. Yes, we become acquainted with the tempter but gradually we also learn to value him in a way. We learn to say: the world that unfolds before us may be maya or similar, but its existence is justified; it has revealed something to us.

And now a second thing arises that can again be described as a very specific feeling in all who meet the requirements of Rosicrucian initiation. It is this: we belong to the spirit that lives in all things, and to which we must pay heed; we cannot understand the spirit more fully unless we surrender to the spirit. And this alarms us! We feel fear as every true seeker inevitably must, a sense of the greatness of the universal spirit immanent everywhere in the world. This greatness before us gives us a sense of our own weakness and we also feel what we or the world altogether would have become in the course of earthly evolution, experiencing our helpless existence that is so far removed from divine existence. We feel fear before the ideal we must come to equal, and before the great exertions that should lead us to this ideal.

Just as we must feel the greatness of these exertions through esotericism, so we must also feel this fear as a struggle we undertake, a struggle with the spirit of the world. And when we feel how small we are and how greatly we will need to struggle to reach our ideal and become one with the active powers at work in the world, when we feel this anxiety, then too, and only then, can we lay aside this fear and embark on the path that leads us towards our ideal. But in really feeling this fully, another significant imagination appears before us. Even if we had never read a Gospel, if humankind had never had the Bible, the following *spiritual* picture appears before our clairvoyant gaze: we are led out into a loneliness that rises clearly before our inner vision, are led to the picture of the ideal human being who experiences in infinite grandeur in the human body all the fears we ourselves taste at this moment. There stands before us the picture of Christ at Gethsemane, experiencing the fear, albeit in vastly intensified degree, that we ourselves must feel on the path of knowledge: the fear that makes blood sweat from his fore-head. At a certain stage of our esoteric path we see this pic-ture, without reading of it in any outward document. Like two mighty pillars, these pictures stand before us on our esoteric path: the temptation, and the scene at the Mount of Olives, both experienced spiritually. And then we under-stand the words: 'Wake and pray and live in prayer, so that you are not tempted ever to stand motionless at any point, but always keep walking forwards!'

This means really experiencing the Gospel at first hand, in such a way that one could write down everything the Evan-gelists described. These two pictures do not have to be taken from the Gospels but can be drawn from within us, can be fetched up from the soul's inner sanctum. No teacher is needed to tell you that you must picture the temptation and the scene at the Mount of Olives. All we need do is place before our souls what can be developed in our awareness as meditation, as cleansing of generally human feelings and so forth. Then, without anyone forcing this on us, we can draw up within us the Imaginations that are contained in the Gospels.

6. The Powers of Christ in Our Own Life

In childhood, to the very greatest degree, we work out of a self that is still directly connected to higher worlds.[11] Up to a point this remains true in later life, though conditions and circumstances change. If you feel later on in life that you did or said something many years before that you only now begin to understand, this is because you were led by higher wisdom back then; and only after years do you gain insight into why you did whatever it was. All this can give us the sense that immediately after birth we were not yet so far removed from the world we lived in before we entered physical existence, and that in fact we can never be entirely removed from it. Our portion of higher spirituality enters physical existence and follows behind us. You can often feel that you not only contain a higher self that must gradually be developed, but that something is already present and so often leads you to grow beyond yourself.

Everything we can draw from within us as ideals, artistic creativity, and also natural powers of self-healing in our own body—by means of which we continually compensate for the harm sustained in life—does not proceed from ordinary faculties of reason but from the deeper powers which, in the first few years of life, work in us to develop our spatial orientation and to form our larynx and brain. These same powers still reside within us later. In relation to injuries it is often said that no external intervention can help further but that our organism must activate the powers of healing it contains, and this really refers to the wisdom present and active within us. From the same source come the best powers for gaining knowledge of the world of spirit—in other words for becoming a real seer.

But now we have to ask why the higher powers we have been describing only work into us in the first few years of childhood.

The first half of the answer is easy: if these higher powers always worked on in us in the same way, we would remain children and not achieve full I awareness. What formerly worked upon us from without must be transposed into our own being. However, there is a more important reason that can help us better understand the secrets of human life than what has just been said. We can discover through spiritual science that the human body at the current stage of human evolution must be regarded as having arisen and developed from other states than its present form. Those with knowledge of spiritual science are aware that this evolution involved diverse powers working upon the human being's overall nature—certain powers worked on the physical body, others on the ether body and still others on the astral body. Beings we call luciferic and ahrimanic worked on the human being to endow him with his present form. In a sense these powers made the human being worse than he would have been if subject only to the powers issuing from beings who, spiritually guiding and directing the cosmos, seek to develop humankind in a straightforward way. The cause of suffering, illness and also death can be found in the influence of luciferic and ahrimanic powers who, alongside beings who wish to help us evolve in a straightforward way, continually thwart this more linear progress. What we bring with us into existence at birth contains something that is better than what we can make of it later in our lives.

In the early years of childhood, the luciferic and ahrimanic powers only have a small influence on us, since they act largely only in what we make of ourselves in our conscious awareness. If we retained beyond early childhood the full strength of our better part, we would not be equal to its effect because the adversarial luciferic and ahrimanic powers weaken our overall nature. In the physical world our organization is such that we can endure the directly acting powers of the world of spirit—which work upon us in the first years of childhood—only as long as we remain, if you like, soft and pliable. We would break apart if the powers that bring about our orientation in space, and the formation of our larynx and brain, remained directly active still at a later stage of life. These powers are so mighty that if they were still to work on us later in this way our organism would waste away under the sanctity of their influence. We must only turn to these powers when we seek to form a conscious connection with the supersensible world.

But this in turn gives rise to a thought that has great significance if we understand it properly, and is couched in the following words in the New Testament: 'Except ye become as little children, ye shall not enter into the kingdom of heaven.' You see, if we properly understand what has been said here, we become aware of this highest human ideal: to increasingly approach what we can call a conscious relationship with the powers that work on us unconsciously in the early years of childhood. We just have to remember that we would break asunder from the might of these powers if they were simply to work directly and without more ado into our conscious life. This is why careful preparation is needed for acquiring the capacities that engender perception of supersensible worlds. This preparation aims to fit us to endure what we otherwise could not endure in ordinary life.

Our passage through successive incarnations has significance for the overall evolution of our human entelechy, which has moved through one life after another. It continues to do so, and parallel with this the earth also progressively evolves. A time will eventually come when the earth reaches the end of its journey. At this point this planet will fall away from the totality of human souls just as the human body falls away from us at death—when, in order to live on, the human soul enters the realm of spirit appropriate to it between death and a new birth. We can discover the greatest ideal here, that by the time the earth dies we human beings should indeed have acquired all the fruits we can gain from life on earth.

The powers that render us unequal to those other powers that work upon us in childhood in fact come from the earth organism. Once this earth organism falls away from the human being, we must by then, if we are to reach our goal, have come to the point of dedicating our whole being to powers that at present are active only in childhood. The purpose of evolution through successive lives on earth is gradually to make our whole being, and thus also the conscious part of us, an expression of powers from the world of spirit that hold sway in us—though unconsciously—in the early years of life. These contemplations, filling the soul with humility but also with a proper awareness of human dignity, can give rise to this thought: that we are not alone; that something lives in us that invariably shows us we can raise ourselves beyond ourselves, grow now already towards something that will increasingly grow in us from life to life. This thought can become ever stronger and clearer in us, calming and lifting the soul, at the same time pervading it with a proper humility and modesty. What is it that we bear within us? Truly a higher, divine human being, with whose life we can feel imbued, knowing that *this being within me is my guide.*

These thoughts can easily show us that in all we do we should seek harmony with what is wiser in us than conscious intelligence. Then from the self we are directly aware of we are led towards a larger self, in relation to which all false pride and presumption in us can be combated and eradicated. This feeling develops into another, giving real insight into the way we are at present imperfect and at the same time showing how we could perfect ourselves: when the more all-embracing spirituality at work in us eventually achieves the same relationship to our conscious mind as it has to our unconscious soul life in the early years of childhood.

Our memories often do not reach back much further than the age of four, while the higher sphere of the spirit works upon us throughout the first three years. At the end of this time a person becomes able to connect external impressions of the world with his sense of self, his I. While it is true that this coherent sense of the I only reaches back as far as our memory does, *by and large* our memory does in fact extend back to the beginning of the fourth year (age three onwards). This incipient I-consciousness, though, is initially so weak that it remains unnoticed, and this is why the higher powers that inform and determine us so significantly in early childhood can remain active for *three years*. In our present stage of evolution, in the middle of earth's span, we can *only* absorb these powers for three years.

But what would happen if it were possible for some cosmic power or other to remove the ordinary I from someone, so that this ordinary I which had passed with him through diverse incarnations was removed from his physical body, ether body and astral body, and instead an I working in harmony with worlds of spirit could be introduced into his three bodies? After three years his body would inevitably break apart! World karma would mean that the spirit being thus connected with higher worlds could live in this body for no longer than three years. Only at the end of the whole succession of our earthly lives will we bear in us something that allows us to go on living with this being of spirit for longer than three years. But by then we will be able to say: It is not I but this higher being in me—that was always there—that now works in me. We cannot yet say this; at the most we can say: we feel this higher entelechy but as yet we have not reached the point of bringing it to full life within us with the actual reality of our human I.

And so at present, in the middle stage of earth evolution, if a human organism came into the world that was later liberated from its I by certain cosmic powers, instead taking up within it an I that otherwise works only in the first three years of childhood, in direct connection with worlds of spirit in which we dwell between death and a new birth, such a person could really only live for about three years. You see, through world karma at this stage of evolution something would inevitably have to destroy this organism.

But this is not just hypothetical, for it has happened in history. The I departed from a human organism, that of Jesus of Nazareth, as he stood by the Jordan at the baptism by St John. And after the baptism, this organism now bore within it, in fully conscious form, that higher Self of humanity that otherwise works on the child with unconscious world wisdom. And at the same time this inevitably meant that the Self connected with the higher world of spirit could only live in this human organism for three years. After these three years, the earthly life of this being inevitably ended.

The outer events that occurred in the life of Christ Jesus must certainly be seen in these terms, dictated by these inner causes, that here came to *external expression*. And here we find the deeper connection between our inmost guide, shining into us in the grey dawn of early childhood and working always below the surface of our awareness as the best part of us, with what once occurred as influx into all humanity's evolution, and was able to live in a human vessel for three years.

This 'higher' I, connected with the spiritual hierarchies, entered the human body of Jesus of Nazareth, in a way that is symbolically portrayed in the dove as image of the descending spirit, with the words: 'This is my son, in whom I am well pleased.'* What does this tell us? We find here the highest human ideal in fact, signifying nothing other than

---

* Translator's note: In the German version, the words, literally, are: 'This is my much-loved son, whom today I have brought forth.'

that the Christ can be perceived in every human being, and that the story of Jesus of Nazareth tells us this. Even if no Gospels were extant, and no tradition told us that Christ once lived, insight into human nature would show us that Christ lives in the human being.

To recognize the powers active in us in childhood means to perceive Christ in the human being. And then we can ask whether this insight also leads us to acknowledge that the Christ did really once live on earth in a human body. Without the need for any historical documents, we can affirm this to be so. You see, true self-knowledge in a seer leads us to recognize, *as human beings in our present stage of evolution,* that powers proceeding from this Christ can be found *in* the human soul. In the first three years of childhood these powers are active without our effort. In later life they *can* be active if we seek the Christ within us through inner contemplation. It has not always been the case that human beings could find Christ within them as they now can. There were times when inner contemplation could not lead people to Christ, and again, clairvoyant insight can teach us this. The life of Christ on earth lies at the transition between a past age when people could not find Christ within them and a present era when they can. And this life on earth itself is the reason why people can find Christ within them as described. For the seer, therefore, the life of Christ on earth can be proven without any historical records.

We could see it like this: Christ wishes to be an ideal that, when we raise ourselves into the spirit, shows us what is otherwise bodily fulfilled. In the first years we learn to walk out of the spirit; in other words, out of the spirit we discover our path for earthly life, the *way* we will go. We learn to speak; in other words, out of the spirit to utter *truth*. Or you could also say that we elaborate the nature of truth from speech sounds in the first three years of our life. And likewise what forms in these first three years gives us the organ for living on earth as our I being, for our *life*. So we learn to walk, and find our *way*, we learn to embody *truth* through our organism, and we learn to give bodily expression to *life* out of the spirit. There is no conceivable significance greater than this of the phrase, 'Except ye become as little children ye shall not enter into the kingdom of heaven', accompanied by that other phrase, 'I am the way, the truth and the life'. Just as the higher powers of the spirit shape the child's organism, without his conscious knowledge, to become a bodily expression of the way, the truth and the life, so the human spirit will gradually become the *conscious* bearer of the way, the truth and the life. In doing so, in the course of earthly evolution, the human being becomes the power that holds sway in him in childhood without his conscious effort.

Words such as these—of the way, the truth and the life— can open the doors of eternity. They sound to us from the depths of our soul when self-knowledge becomes alive and true in us.

Such observations offer us a vista of how humanity and human beings are guided spiritually. Firstly, through self-knowledge we can find Christ within us as the guide whom, since the time when he lived on earth, we can always reach because he is always there in us. And secondly, having recognized realities without the need of historical records we can, by applying this knowledge to them, find the true nature of such records. They express in historical terms something that is intrinsically manifest within the soul; and they therefore form part of the wise guidance which leads human beings to direct the soul's attention to its own nature and being.

7. Knowing Ourselves in the Other

What we experience as our I is only a reflection of it, is only something that mirrors in us our pre-birth I. As reflected reality only, we have a very indirect experience of the true I. What psychologists, so-called 'analysts', say about the I is just a reflection that relates to the real I roughly as the image you see in the mirror relates to you. But this true I—which it was still possible to discover during the period of atavistic clair-voyance until early Christian centuries—is today no longer present in someone who examines his own being in so far as this being of ours is connected with the body. We only indirectly experience something of our I when we enter into relationship with other people and karma unfolds.

When we encounter another person and something occurs between us that belongs to our karma, something of the impulse of the true I enters us. But what we call I within us, and designate with this word, is only a reflection. And pre-cisely this reflected experience is what will make us mature enough during the fifth post-Atlantean era to experience the I in a new form in the sixth era. It is in fact the distinguishing characteristic of the consciousness soul age that we receive our I only as reflection, so that we can find our way into the age of the Spirit Self and will then be able to experience the I again, in different form. However, we will then experience it differently from how we would like to nowadays!

Nowadays people want to regard their I, which they experience only as reflection, in completely different terms from the way it will present itself to them in the future sixth post-Atlantean age. The way people today like brooding mystically on their inner life to discover their real I—even calling it divine—is something that will occur less frequently in future. Instead they will have to become accustomed to seeing this I only in the external world. Strangely, every person we meet who has something to do with us will have more to do with our actual I than what is enclosed in our skin. Thus we are moving towards an age that is primarily social, and in future we will have to recognize that our self dwells with all those others whom we meet. Least of all will it be within us. As physical human being between birth and death I will then receive my self from all kinds of things, but least of all from what is enclosed within my skin.

As paradoxical as this appears, it is being indirectly prepared today through the fact that people are beginning to learn to sense how what they call their I, this reflection, amounts to very little. Recently I mentioned a truth we can discover by examining our own life objectively: that we owe so much of what we are to different people who affected us from birth onwards. There is really very little indeed that we can regard here as our actual I, which as I have said is only present as reflection. To put it somewhat grotesquely we can say that at the time the Mystery of Golgotha occurred human beings were hollowed out, became hollow. It is a significant insight to recognize in the Mystery of Golgotha an impulse that has a reciprocal relationship with this hollowing.

If we are to speak of reality then we must be clear that the place people were still able to discover in themselves in former times—say in the Egyptian and Chaldean king mysteries—must now in some way be filled. In those times this place was filled by the true I, which now ceases when a person is born, or at least during the first few years of childhood, for it still shines in a little in these first years. The Christ impulse occupied this place. Here you see what actually happened. Here [drawing, left side] are people before the Mystery of Golgotha; and here [centre] is the Mystery of Golgotha itself. On the right side are people after the Mystery of Golgotha occurred.

Mystery of Golgotha

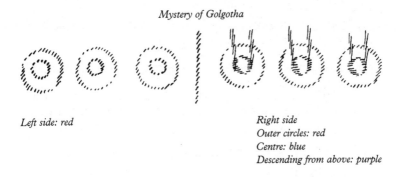

Left side: red

Right side
Outer circles: red
Centre: blue
Descending from above: purple

Before the Mystery of Golgotha, people had something within them which, as I said, was discovered through initiation (red). After the Mystery of Golgotha they no longer have this within them (blue) but are in a sense hollowed out, while the Christ impulse descends into them (purple) and occupies the empty space. Therefore the Christ impulse should not be regarded as merely a teaching, a doctrine, but its reality has to be encompassed. Only when we properly understand this descent in the sense of the ancient Mysteries do we also understand the meaning, the inner truth, of the Mystery of Golgotha. Today, people cannot simply become a 'Christopher' (or Christ bearer) as was the case in the royal initiation of ancient Egypt; but they can do so, certainly, when the Christ in a sense descends into the hollow space within them.

Thus as the ancient mystery principles became meaningless the great significance of the Christ Mystery came into its own. As you can read in my book *Christianity as Mystical Fact*, what was once experienced in the inner depths of the mysteries and made the human being a Christopher was transposed outwards into the great domain of world history and accomplished as an external reality. This is simply a fact. But from this you will see too that the initiation principle itself had to undergo a change since those ancient times, a transformation, for what pupils of the ancient mysteries were directed to seek within the human being in those times can no longer be found today.

The scientific outlook, in which modern English, French or German people are thought to be pretty much the same as an ancient Egyptian, really has to be taken with a large pinch of salt. This point of view completely overlooks essential human characteristics. In fact even outward appearance has changed since those times, but the thing of key importance is what I have described today.

This account also shows why it was necessary for the initiation principle to change. What are we to seek, actually, if we pursue the principle of 'Man, know thyself' in the way this used to be practised in ancient times? What would we achieve by trying to apply an exhaustive knowledge of the initiation ceremonies and practices of ancient Egypt to ourselves nowadays? We would no longer discover in ourselves what was discovered within these ancient Mysteries; and we would accomplish only unconsciously, without any possibility of understanding, what a person became at the fourth level or degree, for instance.[12] Even if we undergo all the initiation rites and ceremonies, all the schooling that led people to the rank of 'Christopher' in olden times we will not be able to encounter and understand the Christ by this means. This was possible in ancient initiation, where people really did become Christophers. But in the course of earth's evolution we lost the capacity to seek in ourselves for the being who later became the light of the world. Today we find a hollow space in ourselves if we seek by these same means.

You will recall a remark I made yesterday—that people today only at most, as I said, begin to sense their I when they make contact with others. People in olden times knew the principle of 'Man, know thyself' in the external world. This is different for supersensible perception, but in the external world in which we live between birth and death with our ordinary state of awareness a person knew and meant something real by this I in ancient times. In more recent times a person only has a reflection of his true I, something shining in to him from it precisely when he comes into touch with others. The other person who is connected with us karmically, or in some other way, brings something real towards us. To put it radically, people today are distinguished by their inner hollowness as far as the reality of their I is concerned. We are all inwardly hollow, and really we should acknowledge this. If we look back on our lives in a rigorously honest way, we will find how much more important have been the influences on us of other people compared with what we ourselves have supposedly achieved by our own devices.

Today people acquire extremely little by their own powers unless they gain knowledge from supersensible sources. On external paths—with no need here for clairvoyant vision—we are compelled to become social because in fact we are only real in the other, in our relationship to the other. And as we move towards the sixth post-Atlantean period, whose germinal impulses can be found today particularly in Russia, this will grow so strong that the following axiom will come to hold true: No individual can be happy or fortunate if the whole of society does not enjoy happiness, just as a single organ in the human body cannot function properly unless the whole also functions.

In later times, our developing state of consciousness will lead quite naturally to acknowledgement of this axiom. We are still a long way from this. So rest assured that you can continue to regard your personal happiness as something possible for a long while yet, even though this personal happiness is founded on a great deal of unhappiness. Yet that certainly is the direction we're heading in, the trajectory of our evolution. It is like having to cough if you catch a cold. Just as this is unpleasant, in a few millennia unpleasant states of soul will arise if one wishes to enjoy some fortune or happiness without others having it too. This developing coherence amongst humanity lies in our human evolution, and is already rumbling quietly in modern social ideals today. This is simply the path that the human psyche is taking.

8. Conclusion: Self-knowledge—
World Knowledge

If you wish to know yourself
Seek yourself in breadths of worlds;
If you wish to know the world
Penetrate your inner depths.
As if in world memory
Your own depths will reveal
The mysteries of the cosmos.

Knowledge of world, knowledge of self:
Back and forth from one to the other
Swings the soul in yearning quest.
Often in a sudden glimpse
We think the riddle might be solved—
But straight away the pendulum
Swings back again from the solution
Creating yet another riddle.
Yet if, instead of looking out
Into the world to penetrate
The deeper fathoms of existence
And if, instead of plumbing the depths
Of inner life to find our own
Eternal being, we seek the self
In universal breadths; seek universe
Within the self—although the soul may not
Immediately come to knowledge
Yet paths to living insight open:
Sustaining the soul, lifting the spirit
And bringing cosmos closer to us.

Seek within yourself:
To find the world;
Seek in the sway of the universe
To find yourself;
See how the pendulum swings
Between yourself and the world:
And then will be revealed to you
Human universal being;
Universal human being.

Know yourself: you'll find
The secrets of the world;
Look into the world: you'll find
The secrets of the self.

You yourself, you human being
Perceiving, feeling, acting:
You are the riddle of the world
What it conceals
Is manifest in you, becomes
Light in your spirit
Warmth in your soul
The power of your breath;
World binds your own corporeal nature
To worlds of soul
To realms of spirit.
World leads you into matter
So that you find
Your human self.
World leads you into spirit
So that you do not lose
Your spiritual self.

Within your thinking dwell universal thoughts
Within your feeling weave universal powers
Within your will live universal beings.
Lose yourself in universal thoughts
Feel yourself through universal powers
Create yourself from beings of will.
Do not end with the far universe
In thinking's dreamy play.
Begin in breadths of spirit
And end in your own soul's depths:
The purposes of gods you'll find
Perceiving yourself in you.

In seeking perceive yourself
And you become real to yourself
Cease to seek, and though
You have your existence, yet
This existence robs you
Of your own being's truth.

Notes and References

Page numbers refer to German editions.

1. GA 13, p. 377.
2. GA 13, p. 378.
3. GA 13, p. 378.
4. GA 13, p. 377.
5. GA 17, p. 48.
6. GA 17, p. 49.
7. GA 17, p. 47.
8. Norrkoeping, 15 July 1914, GA 155, p. 189.
9. 28 December 1918, GA 187, p. 109.
10. When the Anthroposophical Society was re-founded at Christmas 1923, Rudolf Steiner at the same time initiated the 'School of Spiritual Science' as the core of this society. He based this school on a course of studies passing through different stages, which he called 'Classes'. However, he was only able to realize the first 19 lessons of the First Class before his death. These describe a path of self-knowledge that draws on meditative mantras. Thus anyone who desires to engage more thoroughly with the question of self-knowledge should contact the School of Spiritual Science at the Goetheanum, which is represented by local branches in many places. The texts of the Class Lessons are published in the Collected Works (volume 270).
11. This passage is Part Two of a connected discourse on the higher self. In the previous section Steiner shows how powers are active in us in the first three years of life that accomplish far wiser things than we ourselves ever could, developing our

capacity to walk, speak and think. In this second section Steiner returns to the theme of the young child.

12. According to Rudolf Steiner, seven degrees of initiation were distinguished in pre-Christian initiation. Cf. for instance, *Die Welträtsel und die Anthroposophie*, GA 54, pp. 241 ff. (not available in English as complete edition).

Sources

References to Rudolf Steiner's works cite the GA (collected works) volume number of the complete edition of the works published by Rudolf Steiner Verlag, Dornach, Switzerland.

Volumes from which all (newly translated) excerpts have been taken for this edition, together with the titles of English translations where available:

GA 13	*Occult Science*
GA 14	*Four Mystery Plays*
GA 15	*The Spiritual Guidance of Mankind*
GA 16 and GA 17	*A Way of Self-Knowledge and the Threshold of the Spiritual World*
GA 40	*Truth-Wrought Words*
GA 131	*From Jesus to Christ*
GA 143	*Erfahrungen des Übersinnlichen. Die Drei Wege der Seele zu Christus* (no complete English edition)
GA 155	*Christ and the Human Soul* (no complete English edition)
GA 187	*How Can Mankind Find the Christ Again?*

Sources for each Chapter

Page numbers refer to German editions

1   GA 13, pp. 372 ff.
2   GA 16, pp. 39 ff.
3   GA 17, pp. 45 ff.

4   GA 143, pp. 41 ff. Lecture in Zurich on 15 January 1912

5   GA 131, pp. 65 ff. Lecture in Karlsruhe on 6 October 1911

6   GA 15, pp. 16 ff.

7   GA 187, pp. 80 ff. Lecture in Dornach on 27 December 1918
     GA 187, pp. 109 f. Lecture in Dornach on 28 December 1918

8   GA 40, p. 147 (5 June 1922)

     GA 40, p. 297 (October 1920)

     GA 40, p. 289 (27 February 1919)

     GA 40, p. 294 (18 July 1920)

     GA 268, p. 286 (10 June 1918)

     GA 14, pp. 156 f. (Second Mystery Play, scene 1)

     GA 40, p. 223 (Notebook, 1924)